WHY YOU SHOULDN'T EAT YOUR

WHY YOU SHOULDN'T EAT YOUR

BOOGERS

Gross
but True Things
You Don't Want
to Know About
Your Body

Francesca Gould

ILLUSTRATED BY
JP Coovert

G. P. Putnam's Sons
An Imprint of Penguin Group (USA) Inc.

The author would like to thank Susan Punton for reviewing the text.
Also David Haviland and Carl Cutler for their help in the production of this book.

G. P. PUTNAM'S SONS • A division of Penguin Young Readers Group.
Published by The Penguin Group.
Penguin Group (USA) Inc., 375 Hudson Street, New York, NY 10014, U.S.A.
Penguin Group (Canada), 90 Eglinton Avenue East, Suite 700, Toronto, Ontario M4P 2Y3,
Canada (a division of Pearson Penguin Canada Inc.).
Penguin Books Ltd, 80 Strand, London WC2R 0RL, England.
Penguin Ireland, 25 St. Stephen's Green, Dublin 2, Ireland (a division of Penguin Books Ltd).
Penguin Group (Australia), 707 Collins Street, Melbourne, Victoria 3008, Australia
(a division of Pearson Australia Group Pty Ltd).
Penguin Books India Pvt Ltd, 11 Community Centre, Panchsheel Park,
New Delhi—110 017, India.
Penguin Group (NZ), 67 Apollo Drive, Rosedale, Auckland 0632, New Zealand
(a division of Pearson New Zealand Ltd).
Penguin Books South Africa, Rosebank Office Park, 181 Jan Smuts Avenue,
Parktown North 2193, South Africa.
Penguin China, B7 Jiaming Center, 27 East Third Ring Road North,
Chaoyang District, Beijing 100020, China.
Penguin Books Ltd, Registered Offices: 80 Strand, London WC2R 0RL, England.

Design by Marikka Tamura. Text set in Diverda Serif Com.

Library of Congress Cataloging-in-Publication Data
Gould, Francesca. [Why is yawning contagious]
Why you shouldn't eat your boogers : gross but true things you don't want to know about
your body / Francesca Gould ; illustrations by J. P. Coovert. p. cm.
Originally published: Why is yawning contagious. London : Portrait, 2007.
1. Human body—Miscellanea. 2. Human anatomy—Miscellanea. 3. Human physiology—
Miscellanea. I. Coovert, J. P., ill. II. Title. QP38.G68 2013 612—dc23 2012006990
ISBN 978-0-399-25790-2
1 3 5 7 9 10 8 6 4 2

To my mum, Jayne,
and my beautiful daughter, Charlotte

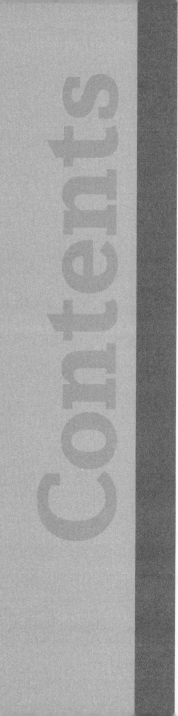

Contents

1
The Skin You're In

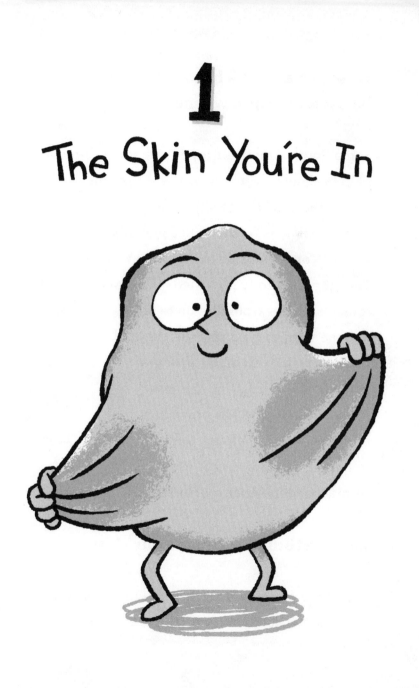

How can an ant's head be used to heal a wound

Some South American tribes use soldier ants to help heal cuts, even today. The skin at the site of the wound is pushed together, and the ant is placed onto it so that its "jaws," called mandibles, dig into the flesh on either side of the wound, like a stitch. Then the ant's body is twisted off so only the head remains. If the wound is quite large, many ants may be used to help seal the cut, and the end result resembles a row of stitches. As unusual as this may sound, this method has proved an effective way of helping wounds to heal. This method also used to be practiced in Africa and India.

Can anything live inside our skin

Yes, there are creatures that can live inside our skin—so get ready to itch! The scabies mite is a tiny insect, too small to be seen without magnification, with a round body and eight legs. Typically an affected human is infested by about ten to twelve adult mites. After mating, the male scabies mite dies. However, the female scabies mite burrows into the top layer of skin to set up a home, and lays between one and three eggs each day. She will also leave a trail of dark-colored marks, which are basically her poo. The eggs and poo trigger an allergic reaction in our skin, which causes severe itching.

If you are unlucky enough to have caught "Norwegian scabies," which is more severe and highly infectious, you can expect to have thousands of the mites living in your skin. Your hands, feet, and trunk will become scaly and crusted, with innumerable live mites hiding under the crusts.

Another potential human parasite is the botfly. A mosquito or other insect deposits a tiny botfly egg onto your skin. The egg hatches into a maggot, which burrows under your skin to grow. At first it seems like you have a pimple, but eventually it starts to wriggle . . . To treat the parasite, doctors place petroleum jelly over the lump. Maggots require air to breathe, so when the petroleum jelly cuts off the supply of air, the maggot suffocates and dies. Once the maggot is dead the doctor can use tweezers to pull it out.

> The egg hatches into a **maggot**, which burrows under your skin to grow. At first it seems like you have a pimple, but eventually it starts to wriggle . . .

Why do we get goose bumps

When we are cold, tiny muscles in the skin contract, causing hairs to stand on end—resulting in little bumps. In our hairier days, lots of hairs would stand on end and trap a layer of warm air between the skin and hair to help keep us warm.

Also, when our hair stood on end, it might have made us look bigger, or scarier. It is perhaps for this reason that we get goose bumps when we feel nervous or angry.

Can maggots be used to clean wounds ?

Placing maggots on a wound may sound rather unsanitary, but it has been found to be an extremely successful way of cleaning infected wounds for patients who have not responded to conventional treatments.

When they are introduced to the wound, the sterile maggots feed on the dead flesh but leave behind the healthy flesh, cleaning wounds in a fraction of the time taken by other types of treatment. The maggots also produce helpful chemicals that kill some of the bacteria that the maggots themselves don't consume.

The arrival of antibiotics in the twentieth century meant the use of maggots fell out of favor, but it is now making a comeback and is used today in some hospitals in the UK. Maggots are currently used for treating conditions such as leg ulcers, pressure sores, and other infected surgical wounds.

To produce the necessary sterile maggots, flies are kept in a sealed room and fed meat, onto which they lay their eggs. These eggs are separated and sterilized, and they then develop into maggots, which are ready and willing to munch on dead flesh!

How can maggots help solve crimes

Insects, particularly blowflies and their maggots, can provide important evidence in the investigation of a murder. Adult blowflies have a great sense of smell, and they find the odor of decaying flesh extremely appealing. They colonize dead bodies rapidly after death, and because they are so quick, the size and age of blowfly maggots on a corpse can be used to measure the time, and sometimes even the place, of death.

In Scotland in 1935, human remains were found dumped in a small ravine. Blowfly maggots were discovered on the decaying bodies. The remains were later identified as those of the wife and maid of Dr. Buck Ruxton of Lancaster. A doctor estimated the age of the maggots, and this provided a vital clue as to when the murders had taken place. Because of these maggots, Dr. Ruxton was found guilty of the murders and hanged.

the size and age of blowfly maggots on a corpse can be used to measure the time of death

The Body Farm in Tennessee is no ordinary farm. It is a center that studies the decomposition of dead bodies using real human corpses. They use bodies that have been donated to science and place them in a variety of situations—such as in a car, underwater, in a wooded area, buried, and so on—to see what bugs do to the corpses.

Why does body odor smell so bad?

The human body needs to keep its temperature at around 99°F (37°C), and one of the ways the body cools itself is by sweating. In hot conditions, the rate of sweat production increases and heat is lost from the body as water evaporates from the skin. Sweat contains a mixture of water, salt, and toxins, and most of our sweat is produced by millions of eccrine glands, which are found all over the body.

However, we also have a different type of sweat gland found under our arms and around our genitals, and these are called apocrine glands. Apocrine glands produce a milky sweat that contains proteins and an oily substance called sebum, which is the skin's natural moisturizer. This milky sweat is an ideal food for the many tiny bacteria that are found on the skin under our arms and around our groins. As a result of the bacteria feeding on this sweat, they produce smelly chemicals, which we smell as BO. The longer these bacteria are left to consume the contents of the sweat (in other words, the longer it takes us to have a shower), the stronger the smell will become.

Deodorants and antiperspirants work in different ways to help the body deal with sweat. Deodorants allow sweat to be released, but they contain antiseptic agents that kill the odor-causing bacteria, as well as fragrance. Antiperspirants, on the other hand, work by blocking the pores to prevent the sweat from being released in the first place.

What is "fish odor syndrome"?

"Fish odor syndrome" is a rare, inherited condition in which the sufferer constantly smells of rotting fish. The smell is caused by a substance called tri methylamine. In most people's bodies, trimethylamine is broken down by the liver. However, this process doesn't work in the case of sufferers, so

"Fish odor syndrome" is a condition in which the sufferer constantly smells of rotting fish

trimethylamine builds up in the blood. The substance passes out of the body through saliva, urine, and sweat, resulting in the unpleasant smell.

This condition can be triggered by a kidney or liver infection or too much intake of the chemical choline, which the body turns into trimethylamine. There is no cure, but avoiding foods that contain choline, such as saltwater fish, egg yolks, peas, liver, kidneys, and legumes, can help to reduce the smell. Trimethylamine is also produced by naturally occurring bacteria in the intestines.

Is it true that we continually shed dead skin?

When cleaning and dusting around the house, you will probably be clearing up a lot of dead skin cells. Every day we shed around 10 billion skin cells, which adds up to around 4½ pounds (2 kg) each year. It is thought that around 80 percent of household dust consists of dead skin cells.

80% of household dust consists of dead skin cells

The top, visible layer of your skin is called the horny layer. The cells of the layer are flat and dead, and rubbing the skin will set many of them free into the air, where they will float around and probably land on your furniture or floor.

Why does the skin on our fingertips wrinkle during a bath ?

Our skin is made up of layer upon layer of skin cells. New cells are constantly growing from below, pushing older cells toward the surface. As skin cells reach the surface, they get drier and thinner. These dead cells lie in overlapping stacks on the surface of the skin, until they flake off or are rubbed off.

Our fingertips, palms, and the soles of our feet have thicker layers of dead skin cells than the rest of our bodies. When we take a bath, these dead cells begin to plump up because they absorb some of the water. If you stay in the bath for a long time, these skin cells will continue to expand until they are no longer able to lie flat next to each other. As a result, they begin to fold and overlap, causing the skin to become wrinkled.

When skin on our fingertips grows back after an injury, does the fingerprint have a new pattern

The swirling, looping pattern found on the skin of our fingertips stays with us for life. When an injured fingertip heals, the regrowth of skin will show the same pattern as before.

In Miami in 1990, police arrested a man whom they believed to be a drug dealer. They found his fingerprints consisted of strange zigzag patterns. They concluded that the man had sliced the skin on his fingertips into tiny pieces, and then transplanted those pieces onto his other fingers. The police came up with a brilliant, creative plan. They took photographs of his fingerprints, cut them up into small pieces, and then rearranged them like a jigsaw puzzle. Using this technique, they managed to re-create his original finger-prints and prove his guilt.

Where do warts come from?

Have you ever noticed someone with a little cauliflower growing on his or her finger? Well, it is probably a wart. Warts are caused by the human papilloma virus (HPV), which causes the top layer of skin to grow too much. Contrary to popular belief, a wart does not contain a "root." A wart may contain black dots, but these are in fact blood vessels that contain blood that has clotted.

> At one time it was thought that rubbing a **dusty toad** onto the wart or rubbing a cut **potato** onto it and throwing it over a fence would help to get rid of the wart

Warts usually affect the hands, but they can also affect the feet. We can catch warts by touching another infected person, or by walking around a swimming pool or changing room where an infected person has recently been. They are easier to catch if the skin is broken.

At one time it was thought that rubbing a dusty toad onto the wart or rubbing a cut potato onto it and throwing it over a fence would help to get rid of the wart. However, warts usually disappear by themselves, although they may take months or even years to go away.

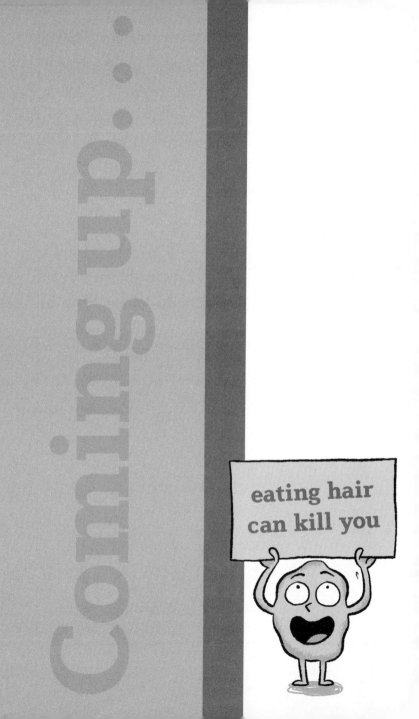

Coming up...

eating hair
can kill you

Hair We Go Again

2

Do bugs live in eyelashes?

Most people don't like the idea that bugs can live on their skin and hair. However, the truth is that many bugs do, and they live with us in harmony, most of the time. By the time we reach late adulthood, most of us have wiggly, microscopic, wormlike mites called demodex mites living in the roots of our eyelashes. If you pull out one of your eyelashes and examine it under a strong magnifying glass—or better, a microscope—there is a good chance you will see one of these tiny mites clinging to the base of the lash. They can also live in our skin pores and the hair follicles on our face, such as eyebrows.

> most of us have wiggly, microscopic, wormlike mites living in the roots of our eyelashes

These mites are cigar shaped and have eight stubby little legs situated at the front of their bodies, so they waddle along fairly slowly. When one reaches a hair, it burrows headfirst down into the follicle. Their bodies are layered with scales, which help to anchor them into the follicle, and their needlelike mouths eat dead skin and oil that is produced by the skin. Fortunately, although the mites eat, they don't actually poo in the follicles.

An individual female can lay a number of eggs in a single follicle. When mature, the mites leave the follicle, mate, and find a new follicle into which they lay their eggs. Each mite can live for several weeks, and mites can be transferred between humans if two people's hair, eyebrows, or the sebaceous glands on their noses come into close contact.

Mites living on our eyelashes are usually quite harmless, and most people are totally unaware of the little squatters in their hair follicles. However, if too many accumulate in a single hair follicle, they can cause itching, certain skin disorders, or an eyelash to fall out. As many as twenty-five eyelash mites have been found huddled together in a single follicle! There are some great pictures of these mites in a variety of poses on the Internet.

What are eyebrows for ?

Eyebrows help to keep water out of our eyes when we sweat or walk in the rain. The arched shape of the eyebrow helps to redirect the rain or sweat to the sides of our face, keeping our eyes relatively dry. Without eyebrows, walking in the rain would be much more uncomfortable. Also, diverting sweat away is helpful because the salt in our sweat can irritate our eyes, making them sting.

Our eyebrows are also useful for expressing emotion. Eyebrows can become very animated when we feel emotions such as anger or surprise.

Wearing animal skins as clothing has often been fashionable, but in the 1700s it was trendy for high-class men and women to wear fake eye-

in the **1700s** it was trendy for **high-class** men and women to wear fake eyebrows made from **mouse skin** brows made from mouse skin. First, they would trap a mouse and then skin it. The skin was cleaned and eyebrow shapes were cut out from it. These trendy folk then shaved off their own natural eyebrows and used glue, made from fish skin and bones, to fix the mouse's skin onto their brows.

Have beards ever been taxed?

Peter the Great (1672–1725) ruled Russia from 1682 until his death. His original title was simply Peter I, but he declared himself Peter the Great in 1721. No one was likely to contradict him, for he was six feet, eight inches (2 m) tall and very strong. He believed that Russia should become Westernized, and because European men were usually clean-shaven, he introduced a yearly beard tax of a hundred rubles (although priests, peasants, and women were exempt). Peter came up with many other unusual tax schemes, including taxes on births, marriages, burials, salt, hats, beehives, beds, firewood, and drinking water.

Does anything eat facial hair ?

There are bugs that will eat just about anything, including facial hair. The American cockroach, *Periplaneta americana*, is a large, brown, winged cockroach, about 1½ inches (4 cm) long. This cockroach is commonly found in the southern United States in tropical climates, and will often be found living in sewers. It will eat practically anything, including leather, book bindings, glue, flakes of dead skin, and soiled clothing. It has also been known to munch on the eyelashes, eyebrows, fingernails, and even toenails of people while they are asleep.

How can hair kill a human

Some people have the unfortunate habit of chewing their hair and swallowing it. This can lead to clumps of swallowed hair becoming stuck in the stomach or intestines and forming a hard hair ball, which can cause obstructions, bleeding, and perforations.

In 1999, a British girl was rushed to the hospital after complaining of stomach pains. Her doctors found a hair ball, called a bezoar, that was 12 inches (30 cm) long, 10 inches (25 cm) wide, and 4 inches (10 cm) thick. It was the size and shape of a rugby ball, and it filled her entire stomach.

A bezoar can be made up of a ball of food, mucus, hair, vegetable fiber, and/or other matter that cannot be digested by the body. In the book *Harry Potter and the Half-Blood Prince*, Harry uses a bezoar taken from a goat's stomach to save Ron's life after he has been poisoned. In the 1600s, it wasn't uncommon for people of high status to be poisoned, mostly through the use of arsenic-laced drinks, and so they found ways to help protect themselves against the threat. They commonly used

In the book *Harry Potter and the Half-Blood Prince*, Harry uses a bezoar taken from a goat's stomach to save Ron's life after he has been poisoned animal bezoars taken from the stomachs and intestines of goats, deer, and sheep. This type of bezoar, which would have resembled a small stone, would be dropped into the person's drink to remove any toxins. Modern research has shown that bezoars can be effective in removing certain poisons such as arsenic when used in this way, as the toxic constituents found in arsenic stick to sulfur compounds found in the hair proteins in a bezoar.

Coming up...

humans
have tails

3
Skeletal Silliness

Why do our knuckles click?

Many people find the noise associated with cracking joints rather unpleasant and believe the sound is caused by bones rubbing together. In fact, this cracking noise isn't due to the rubbing of bones but by gases between the joints.

Our joints contain something called synovial fluid, which is a slippery fluid that allows bones to slide past each other. Synovial fluid contains the gases oxygen, nitrogen, and carbon dioxide. Studies have shown that when you pop or crack a joint, you pull the bones apart and the capsule surrounding the joint becomes stretched. This causes the gases to be released, making the popping noise. A similar thing happens when you pull your foot out of mud.

In order to crack the same knuckle again, you have to wait until the gases return to the synovial fluid, which is why we can't crack the same knuckle two times in a row.

What is the "funny bone" ?

The funny bone isn't actually a bone, it's a nerve known as the ulnar nerve. This nerve is connected to the humerus bone, which runs from the shoulder to the elbow, and it's this bone that gives the funny bone its name (humerus—humorous, geddit?). The ulnar nerve runs down the inside part of the elbow. It controls feeling in your ring finger and pinky and helps to control the movement of the wrist.

humerus— humorous, geddit?

When you bang your elbow against something, you will sometimes knock your ulnar nerve against the humerus bone, causing a sensation of painful tingling and numbness in the arm. There may even be tingling pain felt all the way down to the little finger, where the ulnar nerve ends.

Why do some skeletons have hair?

Hair consists mostly of a protein called keratin, which is also found in our nails and skin. The word "keratin" comes from the Greek word *keras*, which means horn (in fact, a rhinoceros's horn consists mostly of keratin). Keratin is insoluble in water, which explains why hair can become blocked in drains for weeks on end. Keratin is a tough substance that resists the enzymes that usually dissolve proteins. Consequently, a corpse's hair will last longer than its flesh, skin, and internal organs.

Have human beings ever had a tail?

between four to seven weeks of development, **humans** do indeed **have a tail**

Many evolutionists believe that distant ancestors of humans possessed a tail. Indeed, between four to seven weeks of development, humans do indeed have a tail, which is later reabsorbed into the body before birth. A remnant of that tail is the coccyx, or tailbone, which is usually made up of four small bones that are fused together to create one bone at the lower end of our spine.

In 1901, Ross Granville Harrison, MD, who was an associate professor of anatomy at an American university, described a healthy infant whose tail grew very quickly. At birth it was 1½ inches (4 cm) long, and it grew to nearly 3 inches (8 cm) by the time the child was three months old. If the boy coughed, sneezed, or was irritated, the tail would move. The tail was eventually removed, and when Dr. Harrison examined it, he found it was covered in normal skin and contained fat, nerves, and blood vessels. It also contained strands of muscle, which explained how the tail could move.

A man called Chandre Oram is revered in some parts of India for having a 13-inch (33 cm) tail. He has a large following, as many people believe that he is an incarnation of the Hindu monkey god Hanuman because of his tail. People have even reported being cured of ailments after touching his tail. Doctors have offered to remove Oram's tail surgically, but he has declined their help. They believe his tail is due to a congenital condition called spina bifida, which results from the incorrect development of the spinal cord in the womb.

Coming up....

some worms
drink blood

4
Blood and Guts

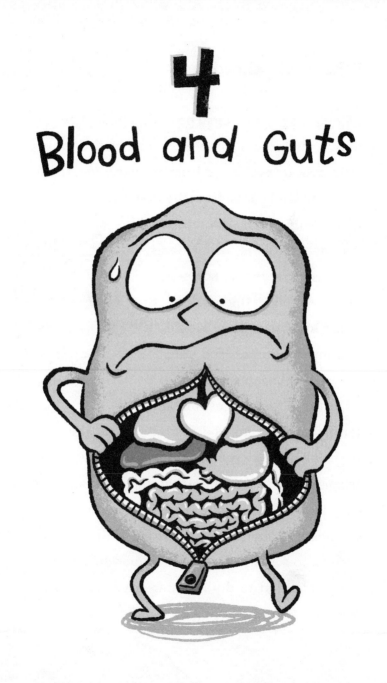

What is bloodletting ?

Bloodletting is a medical procedure that once was used to help cure diseases; it involved draining large quantities of blood from the body. For around two thousand years, from the first century BC until the mid-1800s, doctors would cut their patients, using items such as scissors and scalpels, and then collect the resulting blood in a bowl. They would continue to drain blood until the patient became faint.

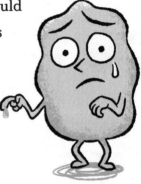

In the Middle Ages, bloodletting would often be carried out by the local barber. This is why the traditional barber's pole is colored red and white—the red color signifies the blood and the white represents the bandages. Members of the Barber Surgeons' Guild were licensed to work with blades, which meant they were qualified to do anything from shaving off your mustache to cutting off your leg.

Perhaps unsurprisingly, it wasn't unusual for patients to die after undergoing bloodletting treatment. George Washington (1732–1799) had nine pints of blood drained in twenty-four hours to help with his throat infection, but died soon afterward. The poet Lord Byron died in 1824 because his doctors literally bled him to death.

How can leeches be used to help severed limbs

From the Middle Ages to the present day, leeches have been used to treat a variety of medical conditions.

In the 1800s, leeches were used to help treat a wide range of conditions, including colds and other infections. Large numbers of leeches would be applied to areas that were swollen or painful. Their popularity meant that some people had jobs that involved collecting leeches to sell to doctors. A leech collector would wade through marshy areas, bare-legged among the reeds, and wait for

> A leech
> **collector**
> would wade
> through marshy
> areas and wait
> for the leeches to
> **latch**
> themselves
> onto his legs

the leeches to latch themselves onto his legs. Around 5 fluid ounces (150 ml) of blood can be lost from each leech bite, so leech collectors would probably have suffered from dizziness and a lot of bleeding from wounds. Also, leeches can infect their host with the bacterium *Aeromonas hydrophila,* which causes diarrhea and infection.

Also in the 1800s, the application of leeches to treat disease became so popular that leeches became an endangered species in Europe.

Leeches are often used today as a tool for healing skin grafts or restoring circulation. During an operation such as reattaching a body part, surgeons find it difficult to reconnect veins since their walls are very thin and they are often badly damaged. A leech's saliva contains substances that

numb the wound and prevent blood from clotting
to keep blood flowing to the damaged tissue.

Do bedbugs really bite ?

Sleep tight, don't let the bedbugs bite! Unfortu-
nately, bedbugs do bite us, but they rarely cause
any harm. Bedbugs are wingless insects, roughly
oval in shape. They grow up to about a quarter of
an inch (5 mm) long, and they are fast runners.
They like to live near where people sleep, which
includes mattresses, bed frames, carpets, floor-
boards, and any other crack or crevice they can
find.

Bedbugs mostly bite during the night. Their
mouthparts are especially adapted for piercing
skin and sucking blood, but we don't usually
notice because their bite is subtle and painless.
They inject saliva during feeding, which contains anticoagulants so the blood doesn't clot
and the food keeps on coming. They also inject

anti-inflammatory agents so you are less likely to feel irritation or get a pimple, which could cause you to wake up and scratch and interrupt their meal! After eating a meal of blood, bedbugs change from a rust-brown color to a deeper reddish brown.

Why do ticks become so attached to us ?

Ticks are small, bloodsucking, eight-legged parasites, which are often found in tall grass, waiting patiently for a passing animal or human to jump onto. The tick uses its mouthparts to burrow into the skin of its host so it can feed on the host's blood. Ticks' mouthparts consist of hooks, which make it very difficult to remove a tick from your skin.

> The tick uses its mouthparts to **burrow** into the skin of its host so it can feed on the host's blood

The problem with ticks is that their bite may pass on dangerous diseases such as Lyme disease.

Which worms like to drink human blood ?

The hookworm is a parasitic worm about half an inch (1 cm) long and creamy white in color. It lives in the small intestine of its host, which may be a mammal such as a dog, a cat, or a person.

Lying on a beautiful beach in a tropical country is most people's idea of heaven, but it is also a great place to pick up a hookworm, as they love warm, damp sand. When we sit or lie on sand, the larvae of the hookworm, which are barely visible, can bore through the skin of our feet or thighs. Once in our system, they are carried in the blood and eventually reach the small intestine, where they take a big bite of the intestine wall and then hang on. They bite into blood vessels so they can eat their favorite food—blood. The adult worms produce thousands of eggs, which are passed out in our poo. If we poo onto soil or into water, these eggs can develop into larvae and then infect someone else.

The first sign of hookworm infection is usually an itch or rash at the site where the larvae penetrated the skin. A light infection might create no symptoms, but heavy infection can lead to anemia, abdominal pain, and diarrhea. Hookworms are native to parts of Africa, northern India, parts of western South America, southern Asia, Australia, and the Pacific Islands. Around 800 million people worldwide are thought to be infected. In countries where hookworm is common and reinfection is likely, light infections are often not treated. Nonetheless, there are effective medicines that can kill the hookworm.

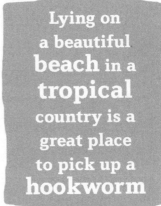

Lying on a beautiful **beach** in a **tropical** country is a great place to pick up a **hookworm**

Why do legs "fall asleep"?

The nerves in our bodies are responsible for every movement we make and every sensation we feel. For every movement we make, nerves send messages from the brain, through the spinal cord, and to the area of the body we would like to move. If our full body weight is on an arm or leg or one is bent for a long time, like when we sit on one foot, the nerves in the affected limb are temporarily squashed. If our nerves become so squashed that the messages cannot be passed through them properly, the limb becomes unable to receive or send messages, and as a result it may become numb and fall asleep. Even after we straighten or move the limb, it may remain numb for a while. But as the nerves begin to stretch back to their normal shape, they will begin to transmit messages once again. This leads to the sensation of pins and needles, until the nerves in the limb function normally again.

Why do we have trillions of bacteria living in our gut ?

Bacteria in the gut help to break down some of the carbohydrates found in bread and sugar, which the body uses to produce energy. They can also help the body to absorb calcium, magnesium, and iron, and help fight off harmful microbes that can cause infection. The bacteria in our colon produce the vitamins B and K, which are absorbed and used by the body.

Some people add bacteria to their bodies on purpose. Probiotics are tiny natural bacteria that are added to food or taken as a supplement to help the digestion of food. Food with added probiotics will contain billions of "friendly" bacteria. These little friends work alongside our own natural bacteria, called gut flora, to aid digestion.

> Some people add bacteria to their bodies on purpose

What causes smelly breath ?

A healthy tongue will be pinkish in color. However, if bits of food, bacteria, and dead cells are allowed to collect between the little bumps of the tongue, they will build up to form a whitish, smelly coating. This coating is more common in heavy smokers and people who breathe through their mouths rather than their noses. It can be removed using a tongue scraper.

Has it ever been acceptable manners to spit at the dinner table

Roman diners regularly spat and vomited at the table and had special bowls in which to spew, although they frequently decided to spit or puke on the floor instead. Slaves had the disgusting job of cleaning up the mess. The puke would have consisted of lavish foodstuffs such as dormice (yes, a rodent) drizzled with honey, which was a favorite food of the Romans.

In the Middle Ages, it was considered acceptable to spit during dinner, but only onto the floor. It was quite proper to belch at the table, but not in somebody's face. Picking one's nose was fine, too, providing the snot was wiped onto one's clothing or the tablecloth.

In Tudor times, Henry VIII's second wife, Anne Boleyn, would puke between courses. Her maid would hold up a piece of cloth so she could discreetly vomit into it without offending her guests.

Can you catch a cold by standing out in the rain

Contrary to the old wives' tale, sitting in a draft does not cause a cold—nor does cold weather, wet hair, or standing in the rain. Colds are caused by cold viruses, of which there are around two hundred. Studies have been carried out that show that people are no more likely to catch a cold as a result of cold or wet conditions. One particular study involved people being sent out for walks in the rain and then returning to an unheated room. They were not even allowed to dry themselves with towels, so they remained in the room cold and wet. Despite these conditions, the group showed no increase in their susceptibility to colds.

If coldness and wet conditions were responsible for causing a cold, we would expect Eskimos to suffer from them permanently. In fact, they do not. The Arctic and Antarctic are relatively germ free, and explorers have reported being free from colds until coming into contact with infected people.

The common cold is caused by viruses that can be passed from person to person. They can be caught through droplets in the air after someone has sneezed, but more commonly through touching an object such as a door handle. For instance, after a person with a cold has rubbed his or her nose, he or she might touch the door handle. Another person might later touch the same door handle, and then rub his or her nose. Bingo! The virus has been passed, and a cold may follow.

The reason we catch more colds in the winter

is not because of the weather, at least not directly. Rather, it is because we tend to stay indoors more, close to other people, and we tend to keep our windows closed, trapping any viruses in the room.

How do vaccines work ?

Vaccines, often in the form of shots, help prevent the illness or death of millions of people each year by injecting germs *into* our bodies. A doctor called Edward Jenner (1749–1823) was the first person to produce one when he developed the vaccine for smallpox. He noticed that milkmaids who had contracted and recovered from a mild disease called cowpox, which caused blisters on their hands, never caught the deadly

Vaccines help prevent illness or death by injecting germs **into** our bodies

disease smallpox. He persuaded a mother to let him inject her eight-year-old son with cowpox. The boy caught the disease and then recovered. Jenner next injected the boy with smallpox and found that the boy was protected against the disease because he had previously been exposed to cowpox. The cowpox virus is so similar to the smallpox virus that our bodies cannot tell the difference. Jenner realized that by injecting people with harmless cowpox, he could protect them from the deadly smallpox.

Vaccines prepare the body's immune system to fight disease by taking advantage of the fact that the immune system can "remember" infectious germs. Each vaccine contains a dead or weakened form of the germ (usually a virus or bacterium) that causes a particular disease. The germ in the vaccine has been altered so it won't make you ill, but the part of the germ that stimulates your immune system to respond is still present.

After your vaccine, some of the white blood cells that are responsible for protecting you against disease respond as if the real infectious germ has invaded the body. They multiply to form an army and attack the bacterium you are being vaccinated against. The memory of this fight will remain in your body for many years, so if the body comes into contact with the same bacterium in the future, the war will be back on and the person will not become ill.

Can a dog lick help heal a wound

When a mother dog licks her newborn puppies, she is helping to protect them against disease. The saliva in her mouth contains antibacterial properties that help to fight certain bacteria that could cause illness. She also licks her own body to keep the puppies free from disease when they eat.

There is evidence to suggest that a dog's saliva can prevent the growth of certain bacteria, however it also contains many types of bacteria that could be harmful.

In the 1950s, research showed that a dog's saliva contained a protein called epidermal growth factor (EGF), which helps to promote more rapid healing. When animals lick their wounds, they are constantly applying EGF, resulting in a shorter healing time. But when doctors applied EGF directly to human wounds, they found it wasn't effective, because our bodies contain enzymes that destroy these growth factors in a matter of minutes.

Why do we get fevers ?

When we suffer with an infection, such as a cold, we may also experience a fever. Fevers are caused by chemicals flowing in the bloodstream that make their way to a region of the brain called the hypothalamus, which helps to control body temperature. As a result of these chemicals entering the hypothalamus, the body temperature rises.

One purpose of a fever is thought to be to raise the body's temperature enough to kill off certain bacteria and viruses that are sensitive to temperature change. However, the fever itself can be deadly in some cases, so we tend to use medicine such as aspirin to reduce it.

a **fever** raises the body's temperature enough to **kill** off certain bacteria and viruses

Why do we shiver?

Our bodies work hard to keep our temperature constant at around 99°F (37°C). An abnormally low body temperature, otherwise known as hypothermia, can be dangerous. So if the body senses that we are becoming cold, nerves send messages from the brain to the muscles, telling them to rhythmically contract and relax—in other words, to shiver. This tightening and loosening of the muscles helps to create warmth. Our blood carries this warmth around the body, helping to raise our overall body temperature.

Which organ can grow back if it is cut in half?

The liver is the only organ in the body that can regenerate itself, which means that if part of it is removed, it can grow back to its original size. The liver is made up of little cells called hepatocytes, which produce new cells by dividing into two and are capable of reproducing at a rapid rate. If a patient were to have surgery to have half of his or her liver removed (which could happen as a result of a tumor, for example), the liver would grow back to its normal size within just two weeks.

If you swallow food while standing on your head, will it end up in your stomach

When we swallow food, it travels along the esophagus (which is also known as the food pipe) and down into the stomach. The esophagus is a tube around 10 inches (25 cm) long, and its walls contain powerful muscles that squeeze the food all the way to the stomach in about two seconds—in a process called peristalsis. Because of these muscles, even if you swallow food while standing on your head, it will still end up in your stomach. However, if you do attempt to eat this way, there is a higher risk of choking, so it's not recommended.

Why don't women have an Adam's apple ?

The Adam's apple is a hard lump found at the front of the throat. It's part of the larynx, or voice box. Both men and women have the same size of Adam's apple until they reach puberty. However, when boys reach puberty, they begin to produce much more of the male hormone testosterone. This hormone is carried around in the blood and causes the cartilage in the larynx to become bigger. Also, the larynx tilts to a different angle in the neck, which makes the Adam's apple more prominent. Girls' larynxes grow as well, but not as much as they do in boys. This growth makes boys' voices deepen as well.

How long can a person live without food ?

Generally, a person can live without food for many weeks, since the body will use its fat and protein stores for energy. Protein stores are found in our muscles, which is why starvation causes muscles to waste away. If a person has a lot of fat stored in his or her body, he or she may live longer than a person who has very little fat.

At the age of seventy-four, Mahatma Gandhi, the famous peaceful campaigner for India's independence, survived twenty-one days of voluntary starvation while allowing himself only sips of water. In 1981, Irish Republican Army inmates carried out a hunger strike to protest the way they were being treated in prison. According to reports, ten of the inmates died, having spent between forty-six and seventy-three days without food.

Without water a person will die within about three or four days

Without water, on the other hand, a person will die within about three or four days, and the size of the person doesn't make much difference to the length of survival.

Is it true you should not swim for an hour after eating ?

When you eat, blood heads to your digestive system to help process the food. Exercise creates a demand for blood in the muscles. During exercise our muscles require more oxygen, and oxygen is carried in the bloodstream. If you eat a big meal and then start exercising vigorously, there may be less blood available for the muscles because it is being used by the digestive system, and this could possibly lead to cramps. This isn't particularly dangerous on land, as you can simply stop exercising and relax the muscles. However, in the water you need to keep moving or you risk drowning. For this reason it is safer not to swim right after eating.

5
Everyone Poops

What is poo?

Poo consists mostly of water, although the proportion of water can vary considerably. For example, the water content in diarrhea is much higher than normal, whereas when we are constipated, the poo will be much drier. Water is absorbed from our poo as it passes through the large intestine (which is also known as the colon), so the longer a poo remains inside the body, the drier it will become.

a **third** of our **poo** is made up of dead **bacteria** that previously lived in the intestines

Around a third of our poo is made up of dead bacteria that previously lived in the intestines. Fiber, also known as roughage, makes up another third of the poo. Fiber comes from plant foods and is the part of the plant the body can only partially digest. The rest of the poo consists of cholesterol, live bacteria, dead cells, and mucus from the lining of the intestine.

Why is urine yellow?

Our kidneys are filtration units that filter the blood so substances not needed by the body can be expelled in the form of urine. The yellow color of urine is caused by a pigmented substance called bile, which is released by the gallbladder into the small intestine. Bile's function is to help break down fats that have been eaten. Urine varies in color from almost colorless to orange, depending on how much water it contains and what we have been eating. If we have drunk lots of water and are not sweating a great deal, our urine will usually be pale, almost colorless. However, if we are dehydrated through drinking too little water or excessive sweating, our urine will be more concentrated and consequently it will be smellier and darker. Eating blackberries or beets could lead to reddish-brown urine, and eating asparagus leads to greener urine and a distinct smell.

Why doesn't sweet corn get digested properly?

If you notice a yellow-dotted poo in the toilet, there is a good chance that the poo contains sweet corn. The outer coating of a sweet corn kernel cannot be digested, because our bodies don't have the enzyme necessary to break it down. However, the inside of the sweet corn kernel, which consists mainly of starch, is easily digested by the body. Undigested foods, such as the outer part of sweet corn, become mixed up with the rest of the poo, which is mainly water, dead cells, and bacteria. Similarly, eating pimientos will produce red blotches in the stools, as they pass through the digestive tract almost unchanged.

What did people use to wipe their bums before toilet paper was invented?

Before paper was used to wipe the bottom, people had lots of other innovative ideas.

Wealthy Romans used a sponge tied to the end of a stick that had been soaked in salt water to clean their bums. It is thought that this is where the expression "the wrong end of the stick" came from.

The Japanese used wooden sticks called *chu-gi* to clean their bums.

Early Americans cleaned themselves by wiping their bottoms with corncobs or scraping them with mussel shells. Yikes!

Vikings used leftover sheep wool.

Sailors used the frayed end of an anchor rope.

Hawaiians scraped their bums with coconut shells.

Early Americans **cleaned** themselves by wiping their bottoms with **corncobs**

Most early Britons wiped their bums with leaves, grass, or balls of hay, unless they were born into royalty, in which case they would have used wool or lace.

Toilet paper was first used in China in the late 1300s. The sheets were enormous, measuring

2 feet by 3 feet (0.6 m by 1 m), and were mainly used by emperors. Modern toilet paper was invented by an American called Joseph Gayetty, who first packaged bathroom tissue in 1857. To ensure that he wouldn't be forgotten, he had his name printed on every sheet. It was called "therapeutic paper" because it contained plant extracts of aloe. In 1879, a British man called Walter Alcock invented perforated toilet tissue on a roll. In the late nineteenth century, people in rural America frequently used telephone directories and clothing catalogs.

How do astronauts poo in space?

In 1969, American astronaut Buzz Aldrin became the first person to have a poo on the moon. He collected the waste

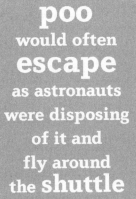

poo would often **escape** as astronauts were disposing of it and fly around the **shuttle**

in a bag that was attached to his spacesuit. Because of the zero gravity in space, poo would often escape from these bags as astronauts were disposing of it and fly around the shuttle. To deal with this problem, the astronauts' diet did not contain much fiber to prevent them from pooing too often.

Astronauts now have special toilets that work rather like vacuum cleaners. When they need to poo, the astronauts fasten themselves to the toilet seat and operate a lever that activates a powerful fan. A suction hole slides open, and the poo is sucked away to be collected, compressed, and stored for disposal.

Why do humans fart ?

On average, we fart about fourteen times each day, enough to fill a small balloon. The reason we fart is to release gas that builds up in our intestines. This gas comes from two main sources: air that we swallow while eating food (mainly oxygen and nitrogen) and gases produced by the bacteria that live in the large intestines. These bacteria break down certain parts of our food, such as soluble fiber, which have not been digested higher in the gut. When these bacteria consume certain types of carbohydrates, such as baked beans, they produce a mixture of gases that includes hydrogen, methane, and certain sulfur-containing gases. The smell of farts comes mainly from the sulfur. The more sulfur-rich foods you eat, the more sulfides will be produced by the bacteria in the gut, and consequently, the more your farts will stink. Foods like cauliflower, eggs, and meat are known for making stinky farts.

Of course, the smell of a fart is only one of the ways in which it can cause offense—there is also the sound. Farts cause vibrations and the sound depends on the amount of gas produced, the speed with which it leaves the body, and also the tightness of the muscles they pass.

In fourteenth-century Europe, it was believed that bad smells could help ward off the plague. Some people believed that farting into a jar and setting the fart free when the plague was around would help to protect you from it.

Has anyone ever earned money from farting ?

In the 1800s, a French baker called Joseph Pujol took to the stage, often wearing clothing that exposed his bottom, and he entertained large audiences with various tunes—all produced by farting. His stage name was *Le Pétomane,* which loosely means "The Fart Maniac." His talents included imitating various sounds with his farts, including the sound of cannon fire. Using a rubber tube, he was able to blow out a candle 12 inches (30 cm) away, just by bending over and farting.

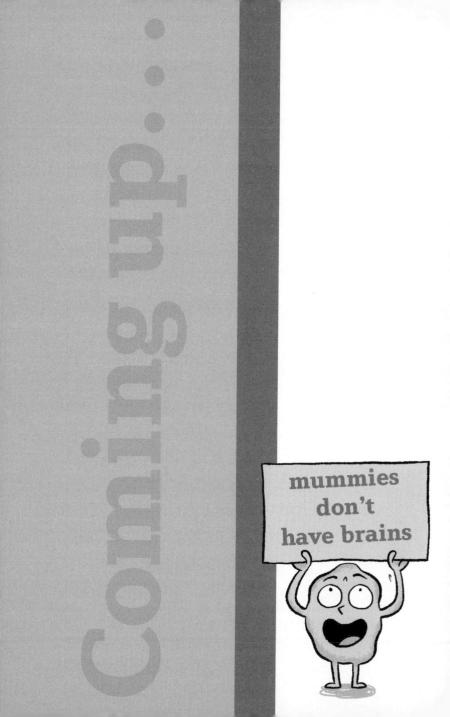

Coming up. . .

mummies
don't
have brains

6

It's All in Your Head

Why does eating ice cream cause "brain freeze"?

Brain freeze is the feeling you get when you eat or drink something very cold too quickly and you get a sharp stabbing pain in the forehead. The reason for this is that there are lots of very sensitive nerves found above the roof of the mouth that help to protect the brain. When these nerves feel something cold, they may over-react and send messages to the brain, telling it to "warm up." In response, the blood vessels in our head widen, pulling in more blood, and therefore more heat, to the head. This rapid swelling of the blood vessels, which contain delicate nerve fibers, is what causes the pain associated with an ice cream headache.

One way to get rid of the pain quickly is to press your thumb or tongue against the roof of your mouth, behind the front teeth. The warmth will help stop the pain.

Why is yawning contagious?

Yawning is definitely contagious. In fact, even reading, hearing, or thinking about a yawn can cause us to start yawning ourselves. Some experts think that yawning helps to stimulate and awaken the body in situations where we have to stay awake, and that yawning may have developed as a means of communication—a way of signaling to others that it's important to remain alert and stay awake in a certain situation.

This theory helps to explain why people who drive late at night yawn a lot.

Another theory is that we have evolved to yawn at the sight of others yawning because our early ancestors used it as part of their social behavior and as a way to help build a bond with the rest of the group. When one member of the group yawned, it may have been a sign that it was time to sleep, so the rest of the group might have yawned in response to show that they agreed. Babies are unaware of these signals, so they don't yawn contagiously until they're about one year old.

Why do we get hiccups

Hiccups are sudden spasms of the diaphragm, the large, sheetlike muscle found between the chest and abdomen that helps to control our breathing. Hiccups can be caused in a number of ways, such as indigestion or eating too quickly. If you eat too fast, you may swallow air along with food, so the body expels this air in the form of hiccups. In other cases, hiccups can be caused by irritation of the nerves that run from the brain to the diaphragm. The "hic" sound we produce is caused by the vocal cords snapping shut after each short, sudden gasp of breath.

People have different ways of getting rid of hiccups, such as holding their breath, drinking water from the opposite side of a glass, drinking vinegar, putting sugar on the tongue, biting on a lemon, or receiving a sudden fright. Some of these methods can occasionally help to get rid of the hiccups, but it's not clear why.

An American man called Charles Osborne began hiccupping in 1922, and continued to hiccup for sixty-eight years, until 1990, when the hiccups mysteriously stopped. It didn't keep him from leading a full life—he married twice and had eight children.

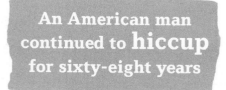

An American man continued to **hiccup** for sixty-eight years

Why do our voices sound funny when we inhale helium ?

When you talk, your voice begins as a stream of air flowing from the lungs through the windpipe (trachea) until it reaches an area of the throat called the larynx (voice box). The larynx contains elastic vocal cords, and when the air passes between them, they vibrate.

One of the factors responsible for the voice's pitch is the speed of sound. In air, sound travels at around 1,090 feet per second (330 m/s). The speed of sound in helium is almost three times faster— around 3,000 feet per second (900 m/s). After helium is inhaled, it will travel from the lungs up to the vocal cords, and the sound waves will travel away from the vocal cords much faster in the helium, creating a voice that has a pitch nearly three times higher.

Without helium, whether our voices are high pitched or low pitched depends on the length and thickness of these vocal cords. In men they tend to be thicker and larger, which accounts for the lower pitch of men's voices compared with women's.

Why do we "jump" when we fall asleep ?

The jerking movements we experience while falling asleep are known as hypnic jerks and can be associated with a feeling of falling. There are a number of theories as to why they happen. One theory suggests that they may be a protective reflex. As we go to sleep, our muscles relax and eventually become quite loose. This loosening of the muscles may be interpreted by the brain as a sign that we are falling (even though we are lying down in bed), so the brain sends a message to the muscles to tell them to tighten up to help us stay upright. Hypnic jerks are more likely to happen when we are overtired or when we have been using stimulants such as caffeine.

Why do paper cuts hurt so much ❓

Our skin contains millions of sensitive nerve endings, and our lips and fingertips have a particularly high concentration. These nerve endings can sense heat, cold, pain, and pressure, and they transmit these messages to the brain. Because our fingertips have a particularly high number of nerve endings, a paper cut to the fingers will generate a greater response than a cut to another part of the body, which is why it causes more pain.

Can the brain feel pain?

Although the brain registers pain felt in the body, it can't actually feel pain itself since it doesn't have necessary pain receptors on its surface. Certain arteries and veins in the brain also lack the ability to sense pain. For this reason, a patient undergoing brain surgery requires anesthesia for the skull, but not for the brain itself. Surgeons can operate on the brain while the patient is fully awake and able to talk and answer questions. Some people undergoing brain surgery have even volunteered to undergo experiments in which their exposed brain is stimulated with electrodes during surgery. When not under general anesthesia, they can even report the resulting sensations to the researchers.

The pain of a headache is mainly caused by pain-sensitive structures outside the brain, such as the many nerves that serve the blood vessels and muscles of the scalp, face, and neck.

How did ancient Greeks use eels to relieve pain ?

The electric eel is capable of generating powerful electric shocks. According to Galen (AD 129–circa 216), who was a famous Greek doctor during the time of the Roman Empire, ancient Greeks sometimes applied

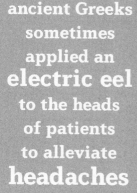

ancient Greeks sometimes applied an **electric eel** to the heads of patients to alleviate **headaches**

an electric eel to the heads of patients to alleviate headaches and to the body to numb pain. The Greeks and Romans also used eels to help ease the pain of gout by making the patient stand on one or a number of electric eels until his or her foot became numb.

Why did ancient Egyptians scoop out the brain when preparing a mummy ?

Ancient Egyptians believed in an afterlife, and thought that one way to achieve immortality was to preserve a person's corpse by wrapping it up in linen bandages in a process called mummi-fication. They went to great lengths to preserve bodies, usually those of wealthy Egyptians, and placed items such as jewels, tools, food, and even pets with the bodies, since they might be needed in the afterlife. Embalmers spent a great deal of time ensuring the bodies were thoroughly ban-daged to protect them from the decaying effects of the environment. However, the bandages did not stop the effects of the bacteria contained within the bodies, and when the embalmers real-ized that the corpses were being damaged from the inside, they began removing the internal organs to help ensure proper mummification. After the removal of the organs, they would fill the resulting space with sawdust and rags, among other things.

To remove the brain, embalmers chiseled through the bone of the nose and inserted a long iron hook into the skull to scrape out the brain. A long spoon would then be used to scoop out any last remnants, and afterward the skull would be rinsed out with water. The Egyptians tried to preserve most organs by coating them in resin and wrapping them in linen strips, which would then be stored in decorative pots in the tomb. But they didn't try to preserve the brain; they didn't consider it an important organ and didn't think it would be needed in the next life.

Can smoking make your teeth fall out?

smokers are twice as likely to lose teeth as nonsmokers

The short answer is yes. Research has found that smokers are twice as likely to lose teeth as nonsmokers. Smoking reduces blood flow to the gums, which means that fewer nutrients needed for healthy gums actually reach them. More generally, smoking reduces the body's vitamin C levels by half, and vitamin C is important for helping gums to stay healthy.

Gum disease can lead to the gums pulling away from the teeth, which can result in teeth becoming loose or even falling out. A smoker's chances of developing gum disease drop to the same level as a nonsmoker's only after a person has stopped smoking for about eleven years.

Why did women blacken their teeth in Tudor times

In the late 1500s, many rich people's teeth turned black because they ate too much sugar, which led to tooth decay. Queen Elizabeth I liked sweet, sugary foods, and as a result she lost some of her teeth and others became black from decay. She filled the gaps in her teeth with cloth to make herself look better in public. It became fashionable for women to blacken all their teeth so it would appear that they were wealthy enough to afford to buy lots of sugary foods.

Ancient Japanese men and women of the nobility lacquered their teeth black to distinguish themselves from slaves. The dye they used contained substances such as iron fillings and tea. They would apply the mixture to their teeth using a brush, until the desired shade was achieved.

Why did people in the late 1700s sell their teeth ?

In the late 1700s, the use of sugar became more widespread, leading to an increase in tooth decay. In response to this, it became fashionable for wealthy, image-obsessed English people to have tooth transplants. Rotten or damaged teeth would be removed and be replaced with healthy white teeth, which were often bought from poor young people, although animal teeth were also occasionally used. A tooth transplant involved taking a healthy tooth from one person and immediately transplanting it into the head of another person, whose tooth had just been pulled. Often, if a good fit was not achieved, another donor would step forward, repeating the process, until there was a satisfactory result. The healthy teeth of executed criminals were also in demand, and there was a consensus that teeth could be legitimately taken from corpses if the person's identity was unknown. There were also stories of teeth being stolen from graves, but these teeth would mostly have been in very poor condition because the corpse would have been rotting. Tooth transplants plummeted in popularity when it was discovered that diseases could be transmitted this way.

Is it possible for a spider to live inside your ear?

Although very uncommon, it is possible for a small spider or other small insect to take up residence in your ear.

In one example, a woman from Cardiff, Wales, went to see her doctor because she was suffering from itching and strange noises in her ear. When the doctor looked inside her ear, he was horrified to see something that, because of his magnifying equipment, resembled a tarantula. It was, in fact, a household spider, which had been there for around twelve hours. The doctor put ice water into her ear and watched as the spider crawled out. Another case was that of a Greek woman in Athens, who complained to her doctor that she was suffering from headaches as well as feeling a sharp pain in her ear when riding her motorbike. The doctor examined her ear and was surprised to find first a spider's web, and then a spider. The doctor said that the spider would have enjoyed its stay in the ear canal because the temperature was ideal for it.

Spiders are not the only creatures that might set up home in your ear. In 1997, a man went to his doctor because he was suffering from pain in his right ear. When the doctor examined the ear, he found it was full of maggots. The man had fallen asleep on a beach a few days earlier, and it was thought that a fly must have laid some eggs in his ear.

> the **spider** would have enjoyed its stay in the **ear canal** because the temperature was ideal for it

Why do we produce earwax?

The ear canal contains glands that produce earwax, which is made up of more than forty different substances, including wax, oil, and dead skin cells. Its main constituent is a substance called keratin, which is a protein found in the outer layers of the skin.

Earwax has various functions, including trapping germs and debris to prevent them from reaching the eardrum and causing an infection. It also contains special antibacterial and antifungal chemicals to fight infection. Earwax protects and moisturizes the skin of the ear canal and so prevents the ears from becoming dry and itchy. The movements caused by chewing, swallowing, and talking help to move the earwax and any other debris, such as old skin cells, dust, or dirt, to the outside of the ear.

The exact composition of earwax varies from person to person, and it ranges in color from golden yellow to tan to dark brown or even black. People may have either dry or wet earwax, depending on their genes and other factors, such as the environment.

Is laughter really the best medicine

When we laugh, our rate of breathing quickens, increasing the amount of oxygen in the blood, which helps healing and improves circulation. This increased oxygen also causes the blood vessels close to the surface of the skin to expand, which is why people go red in the face when they laugh. It can also lower the heart rate and burn calories. It is reported that a hundred laughs will give the body a workout equivalent to a ten-minute session on a rowing machine.

Laughter also stimulates the production of chemicals in the brain called endorphins, which are the body's natural painkillers; they also have the pleasant effect of making us feel happy.

Endorphins have a beneficial effect on our immune system and so help defend the body against illness, which may explain why miserable people become ill more often than happy people.

How can you tell if someone is lying ?

There are a number of nonverbal clues that can help you to work out whether someone is lying. When lying, both men and women increase the number of times in which they swallow saliva (gulp), but this is more noticeable in men because of the Adam's apple. According to research, when people lie, chemicals are released that cause tissue inside the nose to swell. The nose expands with blood—this is known as the "Pinocchio effect." The nose may also become itchy, so liars will often rub their noses to get rid of the itch. Also when people are lying, they tend to touch their faces more often.

Many liars will maintain eye contact while lying to appear convincing, but they may rub their eyes to avoid looking at the person to whom they are lying (alternatively, of course, they could just have an itchy eye!). Other  possible signals include clenching the jaw and tightening of the lips. Stuttering and using lots of "um" and "ah" words can also indicate that a lie is being told. Liars are also more likely to cross their arms and legs.

Some people may cover their mouth with their hand when lying, as if their brain is subconsciously trying to stop them from telling more lies. They might even try to mask the meaning of this gesture by giving a fake cough. Similarly, if the listener covers his or her mouth, this may indicate that the listener thinks the speaker is hiding something. When people lie, they sometimes increase their lower body movement through actions such as shuffling their feet.

Why can't we tickle ourselves?

Tickling relies on the element of surprise to generate the feelings of panic, unease, and laughter that follow. When we tickle ourselves, the surprise factor is missing because our brain knows what the hands are going to do and informs the rest of the brain to ignore the sensation.

In general, the brain pays little attention to expected sensations, such as the feeling of your fingers tapping on a keyboard. However, unexpected sensations cause a powerful reaction, which is probably a survival mechanism that evolved to ensure our brains were paying attention to important matters such as detecting predators.

Coming up . . .

a worm
can live in
your eye

7
Eye Can See You!

Can anything live inside our eyes ?

It's horrible to think that anything could live inside a person's eyes, but there are certain parasitic worms that can take up ocular residence. An eye condition called "river blindness" can be caused by two types of insect: the blackfly and the buffalo gnat, which live on rivers in Central Africa and South America. These insects bite their victim's skin and leave behind the larvae of a parasitic worm, which is then carried in the bloodstream. When the larvae become adults, they breed, releasing millions of offspring that spread throughout the body, carried by the blood. Some victims of this infection may not notice any symptoms, while others may suffer from skin rashes, eye lesions, or bumps under the skin. When the larvae develop, they can set up home in every part of the eye apart from the lens, causing swelling, bleeding, and in some cases, even blindness.

Another potential invader is the botfly. This insect lays its eggs on the bodies of other living creatures, such as mosquitoes, which can then pass these eggs on to humans. In one example, a five-year-old Central American boy felt an irritation in his eye, followed by swelling. The swelling got redder and bigger, and eventually the boy was taken to see a doctor, who initially suspected a tumor or cyst. The boy underwent surgery in Honduras, during which the problem was found to be the late-stage larva of the human botfly.

> When the **larvae** develop, they can set up home in every part of the **eye** apart from the lens

The larva was nearly three-quarters of an inch (2 cm) in length and was removed under general anesthesia through a small incision in the conjunctiva (the thin, clear membrane that covers the white of the eye). You can even find pictures of this operation on the Internet—believe me, it's gross!

Why do onions make us cry?

Onions contain sulfur compounds, which are an irritant to both the eyes and the nose. Cutting into an onion releases these sulfur compounds into the air, and when they come into contact with the water in our eyes, they produce sulfuric acid, which causes irritation. Our eyes then produce tears to help flush away the irritant. Rubbing our eyes only irritates them further because, having touched the onion, our fingers will now have some of the sulfur compounds on them.

British farmers have developed onions that do not irritate the eyes, which are known as "Supasweet onions." Grown in low-sulfur soils, these onions contain much less sulfur.

Why do our eyelids sometimes twitch?

Eyelids are two folds of skin that can be moved to cover or uncover our eyes. The upper and lower eyelids contain a row of eyelashes, which help to protect the eyes from dust and other substances.

Eyelid tremors, or myokymia, is a common condition in which a few of the muscle fibers of the upper and lower eyelids contract irregularly, resulting in twitching of the eyelid. This can be caused by stress, tiredness, or too much caffeine.

Why do we wake up with gunk in our eyes

Day and night, various substances, including oil, sweat, and tears, make their way into our eyes. Tears contain salts, sugar, ammonia, urea, water, citric acid, and certain chemicals that kill bacteria. Blinking helps to wipe away these substances from the eyes during the day, but as we don't tend to blink during the night, these substances accumulate near the corner of the eye. This eye gunk can be solid or sticky depending on the amount of water inside it; the higher the water content, the stickier it will be.

The small, round, pinkish fold of tissue at the inner corner of the eye is called the lacrimal caruncle. It is believed by some experts to be the evolutionary relic of a third eyelid. Cats, many nocturnal birds, and some reptiles, including crocodiles, have a third eyelid, called a nictitating membrane, which moves horizontally over the eye. This special thin membrane helps protect animals' eyes from dirt and debris. Even when this membrane is closed, its transparency allows the animal to see.

Can eating carrots help to improve your eyesight

For generations, people have believed that eating carrots can help improve eyesight, and many children have been talked into eating their carrots for this reason. In fact, carrots can't improve our eyesight, but they can help keep eyesight healthy if someone is unusually deficient in vitamin A.

Carrots contain a substance called beta-carotene, which is converted into vitamin A in our bodies. Vitamin A is essential to the retina, which is found at the back of the eye, and helps to prevent cataracts and macular degeneration, a common eye disease associated with aging that leads to vision impairment or even blindness.

However, eating excessive amounts of beta-carotene, which is an orange pigment, will result in carotenemia, a condition that turns the skin orange or yellow. Many other foods, such as green vegetables, are also rich in vitamin A. A well-balanced diet, with or without carrots, provides all the nutrients we need for good vision.

eating **excessive** amounts of **beta-carotene** will turn the skin **orange** or **yellow**

The mistaken belief that carrots will improve night vision seems to have originated during the

Second World War. England's Royal Air Force spread the rumor that their pilots were improving their night vision by eating carrots, which was giving them a significant advantage over their Nazi counterparts. This was in fact a deliberate lie, designed to cover up the fact that the Allies had developed a new secret radar system, which was the real reason why the Nazis were being outfought in the air. British Intelligence did not want the Germans to discover this radar system and so promoted the carrot story. Many people in Britain ensured that they too ate plenty of carrots, believing this would help them find their way around during the blackouts. At the time, food rationing was severe but carrots were plentiful.

Does the eye have a blind spot ?

We do have an area in our visual field in which we are not able to see objects. Here's a simple exercise to demonstrate the point. Hold up this book at arm's length and close your left eye. Then focus on the dark circle in the box below and slowly bring the book toward your face. At some point, the X will disappear. This is because the X has moved into your blind spot. We are not usually affected by this blind spot because using both of our eyes together gives us a full range of vision.

On the surface of the retina, at the back of the eye, there are millions of color and light receptors, which are called cones and rods. These cones and rods convert light into millions of nerve messages. The nerve messages are then carried along the optic nerve to the brain, which turns these messages into a complete image.

The part of the retina through which the optic nerve passes doesn't contain any cones or rods, so that tiny point doesn't register any images. This is the blind spot.

What causes "red eye" in photographs?

"Red eye" can really spoil a photograph. With piercing red eyes, the cuddly family pooch can suddenly look like a demon.

When we take a photograph, if the subject is looking directly at the camera, the flash reflects off the retina at the back of the eye. The retina contains many blood vessels that are red in color, and this is why our eyes appear red in photographs.

Many cameras have a red-eye-reduction feature, which causes the flash to go off twice, once right before the picture is taken and again moments later when the picture is being taken. The iris (the colored part of the eye) reacts to the first bright light by making the pupil become smaller. Then, when the flash goes off as the picture is actually taken, the camera will not be able to pick up so much of the blood-filled retina.

Coming up....

iron makes
boogers
green

8
The Nose Knows

How does a stuffy nose affect our sense of taste ?

When we have a bad head cold, food seems flavorless. However, it is our nasal passages that are most affected by a cold, not our mouths, where the taste buds are located. So why is our sense of taste diminished?

The tongue contains approximately 10,000 taste buds, which are microscopic structures shaped like tiny onions that can detect chemicals in the foods we eat. To produce our sense of taste, our brains interpret data not only from the taste buds but also from our sense of smell. The nose has a large number of nerve cells, which contain receptors for many different chemicals. Foods such as strawberries and chocolate contain many chemicals that dissolve in the air and are detected by these nerve cells, which then send messages to the brain, where these smells are interpreted. The combination of these smells and tastes together gives us the flavor of "chocolate" or "strawberry."

When we have a cold, our nasal passages may become swollen, and the nose may become blocked because of the extra mucus. Consequently, chemicals coming from the foods we eat won't be able to reach the nerve cells in our nose. Because we are unable to smell these odors, our sense of taste is dramatically reduced.

To demonstrate this point, try this simple experiment. Close your eyes and hold your nose, and ask someone to give you a piece of either potato or apple, without telling you which one it is. Believe it or not, you probably won't be able to taste the difference.

> Close your eyes and hold your nose, and ask someone to give you a piece of either potato or apple, without telling you which one it is

Why do we sneeze?

Sneezing helps our body get rid of potential irritants such as dust and pollen, and it also helps to clear our breathing passages. A sneeze happens when we feel a tickle behind the nostrils, and a nerve in the nose sends a message to the brain. The brain informs the muscles of the abdomen, chest, diaphragm (the large muscle under your lungs that assists breathing), vocal cords, throat, and even eyelids to work together in just the right order to get rid of the irritants, through the amazing mechanism of the sneeze. Our chest muscles squeeze the chest with enough force to shoot air up from the lungs and out through the nose at speeds of up to 100 miles per hour (160 kmph).

Sometimes bright light can make us sneeze—about one out of every three people sneezes when exposed to bright light. These people are called photic sneezers ("photic" means light), and this trait is hereditary.

If you stuck your finger far enough up your nose, could you reach your brain ?

No, because an average-shaped human finger would not be able to pass beyond the nasal passages. Even if an impossibly small finger could make its way through the nasal passages, it would then reach the sinuses. Sinuses are the air-filled spaces behind the nose and cheeks and in the forehead. However, our imaginary finger would then find its route blocked by the cribriform plate, which makes up part of the ethmoid bone in the skull and forms the "ceiling" of your nose.

Why are boogers green ?

The nose filters and warms the air you breathe before it reaches the lungs. It is lined with fine hairs and mucus (snot), which help to trap dust, pollen, and bacteria before they enter the lungs. Mucus consists mostly of water as well as salt and chemicals that help it to stay sticky. Particles that get trapped in the mucus are moved out of the nose by small hairs called cilia, which move back and forth and can be seen only with a microscope. Cilia can also be found lining our air passages, where they help to move mucus out of the lungs.

The body deals with millions of germs and viruses every day. When bacteria start infecting the nose and throat, white blood cells called neutrophils are produced in response. When white blood cells meet germs, they make a large amount of an enzyme called myeloperoxidase, which is green because it contains a lot of iron. The coloration of snot therefore comes primarily from the iron. The breakdown of the bacteria is also thought to contribute to the color of snot.

Is eating boogers bad for you

Doctors have a special name for everything. In the medical community, the technical name for using one's finger to pick boogers is rhinotillexomania.

There are reports that an Austrian doctor has recommended that people, particularly children, should pick their noses and eat their boogers. Dr. Friedrich Bischinger has been quoted as saying, "With the finger you can get to places you just can't reach with a handkerchief, keeping your nose far cleaner. And eating the dry remains of what you pull out is a great way of strengthening the body's immune system."

However, many doctors disagree. They argue that the best way to prevent illness is to *avoid* germs.

Picking your nose ranks up there with spit-

the **technical** name for using one's **finger** to pick boogers is **rhinotillexomania**

ting and burping for grossness and also involves health risks. Our fingers regularly touch items such as doorknobs and phones, which are crawling with bacteria as they are touched by numerous other hands. Touching a germ-covered doorknob and then picking your nose is an excellent way of transferring bacteria into your body. And since the inside of the nose is dark, warm, and moist, these microscopic germs will have the ideal conditions in which to live and multiply, which can lead to infection and illness.

Further, the nose's proximity to our brain creates another potential risk. If the skin inside our nose is broken when we pick it, sometimes an infection can travel straight to the base of the brain and interfere with blood flow, causing a dangerous blood clot.

the end

For kid-tastic facts about animals, look for

WHY DOGS EAT

Gross
but True Things
You Don't Want
to Know About
Animals